The North American Third Edition

Cambridge Latin Examinations
Unit 1   Photocopiable Masters

Editor
Patricia E. Bell
Centennial Collegiate and Vocational Institute, Guelph, Ontario

Consulting Editors
Stan Farrow
David and Mary Thomson Collegiate Institute, Scarborough, Ontario

Ed Phinney
University of Massachusetts at Amherst, Amherst, Massachusetts

Published by the Press Syndicate of the University of Cambridge
40 West 20th Street, New York, NY 10011-4211, USA

The Cambridge Latin Course was funded and developed by the University of Cambridge School Classics Project and SCDC Publications, London, and is published with the sponsorship of the School Curriculum Development Committee in London and the North American Cambridge Classics Project. The work of the School Curriculum Development Committee has now been taken over by the School Curriculum and Assessment Authority.

© SCAA Enterprises Limited 1995
First published 1995
Printed in the United States of America

ISBN 0 521 45845 5

Acknowledgments

The editors wish to thank the authors of each of the Unit 1 Examinations:

Form A (1985–86) **Bill Gleason**
South Hadley High School, South Hadley, MA

Form B (1986–87) **Ed Phinney**
University of Massachusetts at Amherst, MA

Form C (1987–88) **Bonnie Bedford-Jones**
Havergal College, Toronto, Ontario
Mary McBride
Banting Memorial Secondary School, Alliston, Ontario

Form D (1988–89) **David Cullen**
Brantford Collegiate Institute, Brantford, Ontario
Stephen Low
Humberside Collegiate Institute, Toronto, Ontario

Form E (1989–90) **Margaret Doetsch**
Elmwood School, Ottawa, Ontario

Form F (1990–91) **Stephanie Pope**
Norfolk Academy, Norfolk, VA

Form G (1991–92) **Catherine Mori**
St. George's High School, Vancouver, BC

Note to the teacher

This is a collection of all the examinations set annually for Unit 1 of the Cambridge Latin Course from 1985–86 to 1991–92. Each examination has an Answer Key and separate Answer Sheets.

The examinations in this collection have been edited (i.e. questions altered, expanded, or omitted) for consistency. Each examination conforms to the North American Edition of the Cambridge Latin Course and words that do not appear on the vocabulary checklists are glossed in the manner that Unit 1 words appear in the Complete Vocabulary of the student's textbook.

In each Unit 1 Examination both Understanding the Story and Understanding the Background have 35 points each.

The students are given **1 hour** to write each examination in Unit 1. Whenever possible, allow optimum flexibility by giving the entire examination in one sitting and allow students to answer the questions and Parts in any order they wish. If this format is not possible, give Part A: Understanding the Story in one period with a time limit of 30 minutes and Part B: Understanding the Background in another period with a time limit of 30 minutes. Distribute the Latin story in both periods, to assist with the answers.

Teachers are asked to maintain examination security i) by collecting all examination question sheets at the conclusion of the examination and ii) by ensuring that students write all their answers on the Answer Sheets that are herein provided for each examination. If desired, teachers may *temporarily* return the examination questions and graded Answer Sheets to the students for the purposes of discussion, but must then collect all questions and Answer Sheets.

Certificates of merit may be awarded to students who obtain at least 30 points in each of Part A and Part B. These certificates are available, at no charge, from the NACCP Resource Center (address below).

NACCP also continues to distribute new Cambridge Latin Examinations annually. These are available through the Resource Center of the North American Cambridge Classics Project, Box 932, Amherst, Massachusetts 01004-0932; telephone 413–256–3564.

PART A **Understanding the story**

Read the following story, and then answer the questions based on it.
Answer all questions on the Answer Sheets provided.

Caecilius īrātus

Quīntus olim in tablīnō sedēbat. epistulam amīcō suō scrībēbat.
Cerberus prope sellam eius dormiēbat. subitō Cerberus lātrāvit et ē
tablīnō cucurrit. Quīntus Cerberum vocāvit, sed canis iam in viā
lātrābat. Metella tablīnum intrāvit.
    "cūr Cerberus lātrat?" rogāvit Metella. 5
    Quīntus erat īrātus, quod canis eum vexābat. "nihil dē Cerberō
sciō!" clāmāvit, et ē tablīnō festīnāvit. deinde Caecilius tablīnum
intrāvit.
    "cūr Quīntus īrātus est?" rogāvit Caecilius.
    "Quīntus semper īrātus est," respondit Metella. 10
    "iuvenis est," inquit Caecilius, "et iuvenēs saepe īrātī sunt."
tum Melissa tablīnum intrāvit. "cūr vōs susurrātis?" rogāvit.
    "nōn susurrāmus," respondit Caecilius, "sed cūr tū garrīs? cūr nōn
in ātriō labōrās? in ātrium contende!"
    "contendō, domine," respondit ancilla, et ē tablīnō festīnāvit. 15
    Metella rīsit et "Caecilī," inquit, "tū quoque saepe īrātus es. tū
omnēs servōs vituperās. hodiē Grumiōnem et Clēmentem vituperāvistī,
quod tē in hortō invēnērunt, ubi dormiēbās."
    "ita vērō," respondit Caecilius, "sed heri Grumiōnem et Clēmentem
in culīnā invēnī, ubi dormiēbant. servī iterum erant ēbriī." 20
    "servī saepe sunt ēbriī," inquit Metella, "et dominī saepe sunt
īrātī."

sella	*chair*
eius	*his*
lātrat	*barks*
vexat	*annoys*
sciō	*I know*
deinde	*then, next*
susurrat	*is whispering, whispers*
garrit	*gossips*
ita vērō	*yes*
ēbrius	*drunk*

PART A **Understanding the story**

Answer all questions on the Answer Sheets provided.
Answer in complete English sentences (unless otherwise instructed).

1 Where was Quintus sitting when the story began?

2 What was he doing there?

3 What were **two** things the dog did to make Quintus angry?

4 Write in **Latin two** sentences which tell you how Quintus demonstrated his anger to Metella.

5 How did Caecilius explain his son's anger?

6 What did Melissa ask her owners?

7a Which word best describes Caecilius' attitude toward Melissa? On your Answer Sheet, circle the letter of the best word:
    A indifferent   B impatient   C sympathetic

7b Indicate, in English, one thing Caecilius said which reveals that attitude.

7c How did Melissa react?

8a How did Metella criticize her husband?

8b What recent event did Metella describe to justify her criticism? Explain.

9 What reason did Caecilius give to defend his action and to answer Metella's criticism?

10a Which character in the story best demonstrated common sense?

10b Give one reason for your answer to 10a.

11 What does the phrase *dē Cerberō* (line 6) mean?

12 Which **Latin verb** in the passage is a synonym of *contendit*?

13 From the story, give the **Latin** words which contain the roots of the following English words:
    i   dormant
    ii ridiculous

14 Write a **Latin noun** from the story which identifies each of the following characters:
    i   Caecilius
    ii   Melissa
    iii Grumio et Clemens
    iv   Cerberus

15 Which **Latin adjective** did Caecilius use to describe *Grumiō et Clēmēns*?

16 Examine the following pictures.

16a On your Answer Sheet circle the letter of the picture which shows where Melissa was supposed to be working.

16b On your Answer Sheet circle the letter of the picture which shows where Grumio and Clemens found Caecilius.

16c On your Answer Sheet circle the letter of the picture which shows where Cerberus was when the story began.

17 On your Answer Sheet circle the letter which tells the case of *amīcō suō* (line 1):

A nominative   B dative   C accusative

18 On your Answer Sheet circle the letter which tells the tense of *vituperāvistī* (line 17):

A present   B imperfect   C perfect

19 On your Answer Sheet circle the letter which tells the person and number of *scio* (line 7):

    A   1st person singular   B   1st person plural   C   3rd person singular

35 points for Part A

PART B Understanding the background

Answer all questions on the Answer Sheets provided.
Answer in complete English sentences (unless otherwise instructed).

The action of the story in Part A took place in Caecilius' house. Study the pictures below and then answer questions 1–5.

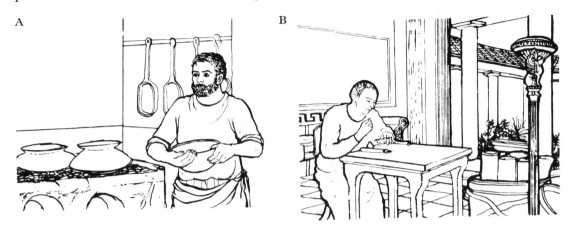

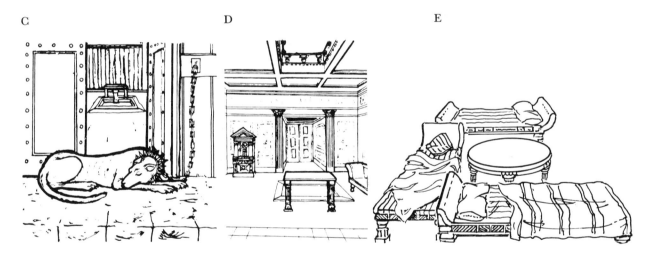

1a In which picture is a *larārium* shown?

1b What was a *larārium*?

2a Which picture shows an *impluvium*?

2b What was an *impluvium*?

3a Which picture shows a *culīna*?

3b Give two clues from this picture which help prove that it is a *culīna*.

4a Which picture shows a *tablīnum*?

4b What is one clue in this picture which helps prove it is a *tablīnum*?

5a Which picture shows a *triclīnium*?

5b How does this room's name indicate how it was used?

6 Study the map of Pompeii on your Answer Sheet. Then, in the squares on your Answer Sheet label the following items:

Label A   Caecilius' house.
Label B   Where Caecilius would have had his banker's stall.
Label C   Where Caecilius would have spent a few leisure hours visiting with his friends or relaxing in the *caldārium*.
Label D   Where Caecilius might have watched a *bēstiārius*.
Label E   Where Caecilius won his case against Hermogenes.
Label F   Where Caecilius might have seen *āctōrēs*.
Label G   Where Caecilius might have gone to honor Jupiter.

7 We do not know how Caecilius' slaves first became slaves. Write two ways in which people might have become slaves.

8 Write three ways in which slaves were different from full Roman citizens.

9 Here is an election slogan that could have been painted on the wall of Caecilius' house:

CIVLIVM POLYBIVM
AED VASPP

9a How do we know that Polybius was a full Roman citizen?

9b What political post in Pompeii was Polybius seeking, according to the slogan?

9c What was one duty he would have, if elected?

9d At what time of day were such signs painted on walls?

9e Suggest one reason for this.

10 In the story we learn that Quintus was able to write, an ability he would have learned in some form of school. Briefly describe **one pair** of writing materials he would use in school when he was learning to write (i.e. what he would write **on** and what he would write **with**).

11 Metella, in this story, behaves as a typical Roman wife and mother. What were two duties or responsibilities of the woman in a Roman family?

12 We know that Caecilius was a rich Pompeian banker. What is one reason we know a lot about his business dealings?

35 points for Part B
Total: 70 points

NOMEN ....

PART A Understanding the story

Answer all questions on these sheets.
Answer in complete English sentences (unless otherwise instructed).

1 _____ ☐1

2 _____ ☐1

3   i _____
    ii _____ ☐2

4   Latin sentences:
    i _____
    ii _____ ☐2

5 _____
  _____ ☐2

6 _____ ☐1

7a A   B   C ☐1

7b _____ ☐1

7c _____ ☐1

8a _____ ☐1

8b _____
  _____
  _____ ☐2

9 _____
  _____
  _____ ☐2

10a _____ ☐1

North American Cambridge Latin Examination: Unit 1 (Form A)

© SCAA Enterprises Limited 1995

NOMEN ....

10b _____
_____ ☐2

11   _____ ☐1

12   Latin verb: _____ ☐1

13   i   Latin word: _____ ☐1
  ii Latin word: _____ ☐1

14   i   Latin noun: _____ ☐1
  ii   Latin noun: _____ ☐1
  iii Latin noun: _____ ☐1
  iv   Latin noun: _____ ☐1

15   Latin adjective: _____ ☐1

16a A   B   C   D   E ☐1

16b A   B   C   D   E ☐1

16c A   B   C   D   E ☐1

17   A   B   C ☐1

18   A   B   C ☐1

19   A   B   C ☐1

/35 points for Part A

NOMEN ....

PART B Understanding the background

Answer all questions on these sheets.
Answer in complete English sentences (unless otherwise instructed).

1a   A   B   C   D   E   ☐1

1b   _____ ☐1

2a   A   B   C   D   E   ☐1

2b   _____ ☐1

3a   A   B   C   D   E   ☐1

3b   i   _____
     ii   _____ ☐2

4a   A   B   C   D   E   ☐1

4b   _____ ☐1

5a   A   B   C   D   E   ☐1

5b   _____ ☐1

6

Ground plan of Pompeii

Unexcavated

☐7

North American Cambridge Latin Examination: Unit 1 (Form A)

PART B

© SCAA Enterprises Limited 1995

NOMEN ....

7 i _____

ii _____ ☐ 2

8 i _____

ii _____

iii _____ ☐ 3

9a _____ ☐ 1

9b _____ ☐ 1

9c _____ ☐ 1

9d _____ ☐ 1

9e _____ ☐ 1

10 i _____

_____

ii _____

_____ ☐ 4

11 i _____

ii _____ ☐ 2

12 _____ ☐ 1

/35 **points for Part B**

/35 +   /35 =   /70 **points total**

North American Cambridge Latin Examination: Unit 1 (Form A)

© SCAA Enterprises Limited 1995

Answer Key

Each question is worth 1 point unless otherwise indicated.

PART A Understanding the story

1. Quintus was sitting in his study.
2. He was writing a letter to his friend.
3. Any two of: The dog barked.
   The dog ran out of the study.
   The dog did not come when called.
   The dog barked / was barking in the street. (2 points)
4. *Quintus clamavit, "nihil de Cerbero scio."* (1) and *Quintus e tablino festinavit.* (1) (2 points total)
5. Caecilius said that Quintus was angry because he was young (1), and young people are often angry (1). (2 points total)
6. Melissa asked her owners why they were whispering.
7a. B (impatient)
7b. Any one of: "Why are you gossiping?" "Why aren't you working in the atrium?" "Hurry to the atrium."
7c. She hurried out of the study to the atrium, where her work was.
8a. She said he was often angry and/or scolded all the slaves.
8b. That day Caecilius had scolded Grumio and Clemens (1). They found him asleep in the garden (1). (2 points total)
9. Any two of: Caecilius said he had found them asleep the day before. He had found them drunk in the kitchen. The slaves were drunk again. (2 points)
10a. Metella
10b. She recognized that both Quintus and Caecilius were often angry. OR She recognized that slaves were often drunk, and their masters angry. (2 points)
11. about Cerberus
12. *festinavit* (lines 7 & 15)
13. i *dormiebat* (line 2); *dormiebas* (line 18); *dormiebant* (line 20)
    ii *risit* (line 16)
14. i *domine* (line 15); *domini* (line 21)
    ii *ancilla* (line 15)
    iii *servos* (line 17); *servi* (lines 20 & 21)   (the plural form is obligatory)
    iv *canis* (line 3)
15. *ebrii* (line 20)
16a. Picture C
16b. Picture B
16c. Picture E
17. B (dative case)
18. C (perfect tense)
19. A (1st person singular)

35 points for Part A

PART B Understanding the background

- **1a** Picture D
- **1b** The *lararium* was a family shrine (set up in the atrium, where the *lares*, household gods, were kept). The *lares* were guardian spirits of the family (other details in Unit 1 Workbook, p. 20).
- **2a** Picture D
- **2b** The *impluvium* was a pool of water under an opening in the roof.
- **3a** Picture A
- **3b** Any two of: Pots/stove/bowls/pans hanging indicate this room is a *culina*. (2 points)
- **4a** Picture B
- **4b** Any one item: Table/scrolls/opening to the peristyle indicate this room is a *tablinum*.
- **5a** Picture E
- **5b** *Triclinium* means three (*tri*) dining couches arranged around a table (for reclining).
- **6** Clockwise from bottom left (*basilica*): E, B, G, A, C, D, F   (7 points)
- **7** Any two of: Slaves might have been captured in war.
  Slaves might have been kidnaped by pirates.
  Slaves might have been born into slave-families.   (2 points)
- **8** Any three of: Slaves could not make their own decisions.
  Slaves could not marry.
  Slaves could not own personal possessions.
  Slaves could be bought or sold.
  Menial work was usually done by slaves.
  Slaves were not protected by the law.   (3 points)
- **9a** He has three names. OR You cannot run for public office unless you are a citizen.
- **9b** aedile
- **9c** Any one of: supervising public markets, police force, baths, places of public entertainment, water supply, sewers; spending taxes wisely, seeing public services were efficiently run
- **9d** Signs were painted at night.
- **9e** There would be less trouble from rivals OR less congestion on roads and sidewalks.
- **10** Either this pair:
  wax tablet [*tabula*] (1) – thin coating of wax on a wooden tablet (1)
  pen [*stilus*] (1) – a pen made of metal, bone, or ivory (1)
  or this pair:
  papyrus (1) – made from reed plant fibers (1)
  quill pen (1) – pen made from a reed or goose quill, using ink (1)   (4 points total)
- **11** Any two of: manage household, supervise slaves, prepare for social occasions/guests   (2 points)
- **12** His business accounts were discovered when his house was excavated.

35 points for Part B
Total: 70 points

PART A Understanding the story

Read the following story, and then answer the questions based on it.
Answer all questions on the Answer Sheets provided.

cēna

Caecilius et Metella et Quīntus in triclīniō recumbēbant et cēnābant.
pāvō pulcherrimus erat in mēnsā. cēna omnēs dēlectābat.
    Grumiō triclīnium intrāvit.
    "Grumiō!" clāmāvit Caecilius. "pāvō est optimus!"
    "ego, domine, tibi grātiās agō," respondit Grumiō, "sed Melissa   5
pāvōnem vōbīs parāvit." Caecilius et Quīntus Melissam valdē
laudāvērunt, sed Metella tacuit.
    Melissa triclīnium intrāvit.
    "cupitisne vīnum?" rogāvit Melissa. Caecilius et Quīntus vīnum nōn
cupīvērunt, sed Metella dīxit, "ego, quod cēna mē nōn dēlectat,   10
multum vīnum cupiō."
    Caecilius laetus nōn erat, et uxōrem vituperāvit. Metella nihil
cūrāvit et multum vīnum bibit.
    Melissa, postquam omnēs cēnāvērunt et bibērunt, suāviter cantāvit.
Melissa virōs dēlectāvit, sed Metellam nōn dēlectāvit.   15
    subitō Metella surrēxit et clāmāvit, "audīte, omnēs!" et vehementer
cantāvit. Cerberus lātrāvit. Grumiō rīsit. Quīntus erat attonitus.
Caecilius erat īrātissimus.
    "Metella, cūr nimium bibistī?" rogāvit Caecilius. tum Caecilius exiit
et ad tablīnum festīnāvit.   20

pāvō: pāvōnem	*peacock*
nihil cūrāvit	*didn't care*
lātrāvit	*barked*
attonitus	*astonished*
nimium	*too much*

PART A Understanding the story

Answer all questions on the Answer Sheets provided.
Answer in complete English sentences (unless otherwise instructed).

1   Where were Caecilius and his family at the beginning of this story?

2   Write the **two Latin** verbs which describe what they were doing there.

3   What was the main course of the dinner?

4a Write the **Latin** words with which Caecilius expressed his opinion of the main course.

4b To whom were these words addressed?

5a Who really prepared the main course?

5b How do we know this?

6   Why do you think Caecilius scolded Metella?

7   How did Metella react to Caecilius' scolding?

8   Who liked Melissa's song?

9a Who did not like Melissa's song?

9b What did this person do to show that he/she disliked it? (3 details)

10 Describe the reaction of the following to Metella's performance:
      i Grumio   ii Quintus   iii Cerberus   iv Caecilius

11a What did Caecilius ask Metella at the end of the story?

11b Why do you think Caecilius did not wait for Metella's answer?

12 From the story find an example of a superlative adjective.

13a Write the **Latin** word which describes how Melissa sang.

13b Write the **Latin** word which describes Metella's performance.

14 Translate into English: *"ego, domine, tibi grātiās agō,"* respondit Grumiō. (line 5)

15 Translate into English: *"cupitisne vīnum?"* rogāvit Melissa. (line 9)

16 Which **Latin** words in this story provide the root of the following English words?
      i imbibe   ii response   iii interrogative   iv multitude

17 On your Answer Sheet circle the Latin adjective which best describes Metella in the story:
      avāra   contenta   īrāta   laeta

35 points for Part A

North American Cambridge Latin Examination: Unit 1 (Form B)

PART B Understanding the background

Answer all questions on the Answer Sheets provided.
Answer in complete English sentences (unless otherwise instructed).

1a The story refers to the main course of Caecilius' dinner. What would the first course have been?

1b What would dessert have been?

2 In the story, we meet Melissa, a slave girl.

2a What were **two** disadvantages of being a slave in Roman times?

2b What was one advantage of being a slave like Melissa?

Metella   Melissa

3 Study the plan of the Roman house below and then, on your Answer Sheet, label the following items.

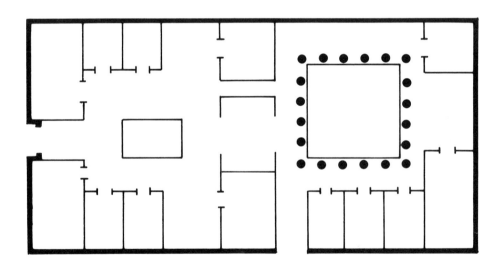

Label A: *impluvium*
Label B: *tablīnum*
Label C: *ātrium*
Label D: *peristȳlium*
Label E: summer *triclīnium*

North American Cambridge Latin Examination: Unit 1 (Form B)

© SCAA Enterprises Limited 1995

4 On your Answer Sheet match the following teachers and educators in column I with their correct tasks in column II:

I   II

ludī magister   A   a slave who escorted students to school
paedagōgus   B   taught advanced literature and public speaking
grammaticus   C   taught basic reading and writing skills
rhētor   D   taught the works of famous Greek and Roman writers

5 What kind of teacher, of those named in 4 above, was Theodorus, who taught Quintus and his friend Alexander in Pompeii?

6 Study the picture below and then, in the squares on your Answer Sheet, label the following writing materials.

Label A: inkwell   Label D: *stilus*
Label B: writing tablet   Label E: *papyrus* scroll
Label C: pen

7 Describe a writing tablet.

8a From what material might a *stilus* be made?

8b Explain how both ends of a *stilus* were used.

9 Where did *papyrus* come from?

10 Name two famous writers studied in Roman schools.

11 Give two reasons why a Roman would have wanted to learn Greek.

12 On your Answer Sheet circle the letter of the subject which was *not* taught in Roman schools:

A   literature   B   Greek   C   science   D   public speaking
E   writing

13 Where did a Roman learn technical skills (e.g. pot-making)?

14 Explain what each of the following men did:

    i   a *duovir*   ii   a *rētiārius*   iii   an *ōstiārius*

35 points for Part B
Total: 70 points

NOMEN ....

PART A Understanding the story

Answer all questions on these sheets.
Answer in complete English sentences (unless otherwise instructed).

1 _____ ☐1

2 Latin words:
  i _____
  ii _____ ☐2

3 _____ ☐1

4a Latin words: _____ ☐1

4b _____ ☐1

5a _____ ☐1

5b _____ ☐1

6 _____
 _____ ☐1

7 _____ ☐1

8 _____ ☐1

9a _____ ☐1

9b _____
 _____
 _____ ☐3

10 i Grumio _____ ☐1
  ii Quintus _____ ☐1
  iii Cerberus _____ ☐1
  iv Caecilius _____ ☐1

11a _____ ☐1

North American Cambridge Latin Examination: Unit 1 (Form B)

© SCAA Enterprises Limited 1995

NOMEN ....

11b _____
_____ ☐1

12 Latin superlative adjective: _____ ☐1

13a Latin word: _____ ☐1

13b Latin word: _____ ☐1

14 _____ ☐3

15 _____ ☐3

16 i _____ ☐1

   ii _____ ☐1

   iii _____ ☐1

   iv _____ ☐1

17 *avāra*   *contenta*   *īrāta*   *laeta* ☐1

/35 **points for Part A**

NOMEN ....

PART B **Understanding the background**

Answer all questions on these sheets.
Answer in complete English sentences (unless otherwise instructed).

1a _____ ☐1

1b _____ ☐1

2a i _____
   ii _____ ☐2

2b _____ ☐1

3
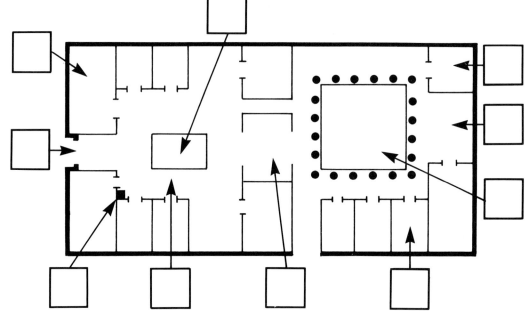

☐5

4 *ludī magister*   A   B   C   D
   paedagōgus   A   B   C   D
   grammaticus   A   B   C   D
   rhētor   A   B   C   D   ☐4

5 _____ ☐1

NOMEN ....

6

☐ 5

7 _____

☐ 2

8a _____ ☐ 1

8b _____

☐ 2

9 _____

☐ 1

10 i _____
     ii _____

☐ 2

11 i _____

     ii _____

☐ 2

12   A   B   C   D   E   ☐ 1

13 _____

☐ 1

North American Cambridge Latin Examination: Unit 1 (Form B)

NOMEN ....

14 i _____

 _____

 ii _____

 _____

 iii _____

 _____ ☐ 3

/35 **points for Part B**

/35 + /35 = /70 **points total**

Answer Key

Each question is worth 1 point unless otherwise indicated.

PART A Understanding the story

1 Caecilius and his family were in the dining room.

2 i *recumbebant* ii *cenabant* (2 points)

3 The main course of the dinner was peacock.

4a *"pavo est optimus!"*

4b These words were addressed to Grumio.

5a Melissa really prepared the main course.

5b Grumio told this to Caecilius.

6 Caecilius scolded Metella because she said she wanted to drink lots of wine/perhaps because she insulted Melissa when she said she did not like the dinner.

7 Metella did not care at all/drank lots of wine.

8 The men (Caecilius and Quintus) liked Melissa's song.

9a Metella did not like Melissa's song.

9b Metella suddenly got up; she shouted "Listen everybody!"; and she sang loudly. (3 points)

10 i Grumio laughed (smiled).
 ii Quintus was astonished.
 iii Cerberus barked.
 iv Caecilius was very angry. (4 points total)

11a Caecilius asked Metella why she drank too much (wine).

11b Caecilius sensed that his wife was jealous of Melissa/perhaps she was still ignoring him (cf. lines 12–13: *nihil curavit*), and he knew she would not answer him.

12 *pulcherrimus* (line 2), *optimus* (line 4), *iratissimus* (line 18)

13a *suaviter* (line 14)

13b *vehementer* (line 16)

14 "I thank you (1), Master (1)," Grumio replied (1). (3 points total)

15 "Do you want (some) wine (2)?" Melissa asked (1). (3 points total)

16 i *bibit* (line 13), or *biberunt* (line 14), or *bibisti* (line 19)
 ii *respondit* (line 5)
 iii *rogavit* (lines 9 & 19)
 iv *multum* (lines 11 & 13)

17 *īrāta*

35 points for Part A

PART B Understanding the background

1a The first course would have been light dishes like eggs and fish.

1b Any one of: Dessert would have been fruit, nuts, and cheese.

2a Any two of: Slaves were considered as property, not persons. Slaves could not marry. Slaves could not own property. Slaves could not be protected by the law, etc. (2 points)

2b Slaves were provided with room and board. With kind masters, such as Caecilius, they were treated well.

3

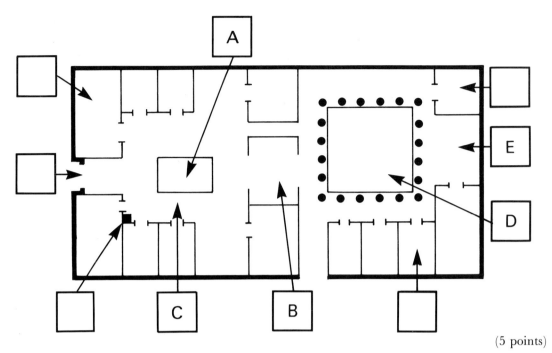

(5 points)

4   *ludi magister*   C
    paedagogus   A
    grammaticus   D
    rhetor   B   (4 points)

5   Theodorus was a *rhetor*.

6

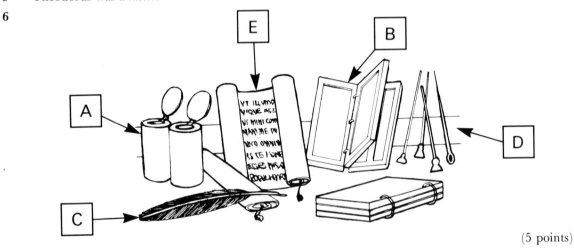

(5 points)

7   Any two details: A writing tablet was a slab of wood coated with a film of wax; sometimes several tablets were strung together to make a writing-book.   (2 points)

8a A *stilus* was made from a thin stick of any one of metal, bone, or ivory.

8b The pointed end was used to inscribe letters on the wax surface of the tablet; the opposite (flat, wider) end was used to flatten out (erase/rub) letters inscribed on the wax surface.   (2 points)

9   *Papyrus*, the material, was made from the fibers of papyrus, the reed, which grew along the banks of the river Nile in Egypt.

10 Homer, Aeschylus, Sophocles, Euripides, or Vergil (any two, at 1 point each)

11 i   Knowledge of Greek would have opened for a Roman the riches of Greek literature and philosophy, which were highly admired by the Romans.

    ii Knowledge of Greek would have been of practical value if a young Roman had ambitions to be a merchant or government official in parts of the Roman Empire where Greek was widely spoken (i.e. provinces of the Eastern Mediterranean).   (2 points total)

12   C (science)

13   A Roman learned technical skills like pot-making as an apprentice to a skilled worker.

14   i A *duovir* was one of two public officials of this name. He was a senior magistrate hearing evidence and giving judgments in court.
      ii A *rētiārius* was the "net" gladiator who fought with a net and trident.
      iii An *ōstiārius* was the doorkeeper who collected admission fees at the baths.   (3 points total)

35 points for Part B
Total: 70 points

PART A — Understanding the story

Read the following story, and then answer the questions based on it.
Answer all questions on the Answer Sheets provided.

duo servī

nēmō in forō negōtium agit, quod omnēs Pompēiānī sunt ōtiōsī.
argentārius argentāriam nōn aperit. hodiē iūdicēs in basilicā nōn
sedent. servī dominīs cibum nōn emunt. pistōrēs pānem nōn vēndunt.
tōnsōrēs barbās nōn tondent. cīvēs thermās nōn vīsitant. magna turba
per viās currit. nūntiī spectāculum in amphitheātrō nūntiant: 5
   "deī nōbīs favent! hodiē trīgintā gladiātōrēs in arēnā pugnant! venīte
nunc ad spectāculum! vidēte bēstiāriōs audācissimōs et bēstiās ferōcēs!"
   Metella et Caecilius et Quīntus amphitheātrum petunt. Grumiō et
Clēmēns tamen in vīllā manent. in hortō sedent et garriunt.
   "quid tū herī fēcistī, Clēmēns?" rogat Grumiō.   10
   "herī ego et amīca mea fābulam in theātrō vīdimus. nōs āctōrēs in
scaenā spectāvimus. in fābulā servus senem dēcipiēbat, quod servus et
iuvenis pecūniam cupiēbant. ille senex dīves erat: fīliam pulchram
quoque habēbat. iuvenis, postquam hanc puellam cōnspexit, statim
eam amāvit et senī pecūniam reddidit. tum omnēs erant laetī."   15
   "quis tēcum ad theātrum iit?" rogat Grumiō.
   "Poppaea, amīca mea, mēcum fābulam spectāvit," respondet
Clēmēns.
   "Poppaea!" exclāmat Grumiō attonitus. "amīca tua! mendāx es.
Poppaea est amīca mea."   20
   "minimē, amīce," respondet Clēmēns. "Poppaea mē amat, quod ego
in forō Caecilium fortiter servāvī. nunc Poppaea mē Clēmentem valdē
amat. Poppaea tē Lūcium Spurium Pompōniānum nōn amat. valē."

nēmō	*no one*	amat	*loves, falls in love with*
ōtiōsus	*on holiday*	tēcum	*with you*
argentāria	*banker's stall*	attonitus	*astonished*
aperit	*opens*		
pānis: pānem	*bread*		
barba	*beard*		
tondet	*trims*		
deus	*god*		
trīgintā	*thirty*		
audācissimus	*very bold*		
garrit	*chats*		
scaena	*stage*		
dēcipit	*deceives*		
dīves	*rich*		

PART A **Understanding the story**

Answer all questions on the Answer Sheets provided.
Answer in complete English sentences (unless otherwise instructed).

1 Why is nobody working in the forum?

2 What usual activities are *not* taking place today? (six details)

3 In this story, how is the show being publicized?

4 Which **Latin adjectives** make the hunt of wild animals sound like an exciting part of the day?

5 Why are Grumio and Clemens alone in the house when they start their conversation?

6 Translate the following sentence into English (line 10):
 "*quid tū herī fēcistī?*" *rogat Grumiō.*

7a Where was Clemens the day before?

7b Who was with him?

8 Who were the main characters in the play which Clemens saw? (four characters)

9 What was the sequence of *action* in the play?

10 After Grumio hears about Clemens' day at the theater, which question still remains unanswered for Grumio?

11 In line 19, why does Grumio call Clemens a liar?

12 Why, according to Clemens, did Poppaea jilt Grumio for Clemens?

13 From this story and others you have read in Unit 1, explain why (in line 23) Clemens reminds Grumio of his alias, Lucius Spurius Pomponianus.

14 In the story find an example of each of the following:
 i a superlative adjective
 ii a noun that is dative plural
 iii a verb in the imperfect tense
 iv a verb in the perfect tense

15 In the story, find the **Latin** root word for each of the following English derivatives:
 i inconspicuous ii senile iii exclaim iv pulchritude

35 points for Part A

PART B Understanding the background

Answer all questions on the Answer Sheets provided.
Answer in complete English sentences (unless otherwise instructed).

1 Name **three** purposes for which the forum was used.

2 Where would Pompeians have found written information publicizing gladiatorial shows?

3 Name one leisure-time activity for Pompeian citizens on a normal day when no gladiatorial shows or plays were being held.

4 Name **two** items which an ordinary Pompeian citizen would have been sure to take along when he or she set out to spend a day at the theater or amphitheater.

5a What is shown in the pictures below?

5b Who would use these?

6 How many spectators could be seated in the large theater at Pompeii?

7 Describe a pantomime production as presented on the Roman stage.

8 Name one famous Roman author of comedies.

9 What might the presenter of the gladiatorial game have provided for the comfort of the spectators?

10 Identify the type of gladiator shown in each of the pictures below:

i ii

11 *"deī nōbīs favent!"* (line 6). The gods played an important role in the lives of the Pompeians.

11a Name two native Roman gods or goddesses who had temples in Pompeii.

11b Where did Pompeians worship when they were at home?

11c Name the Egyptian goddess who had a temple in Pompeii.

12 Grumio and Clemens talked in the garden. Name two rooms of a Roman house which might have opened onto the *peristȳlium*. (Answer in English or in Latin.)

13 Describe **three** special features of the garden and its *peristȳlium*.

14 The pictures below show common objects used in everyday life in Pompeii. For what purpose would each have been used?

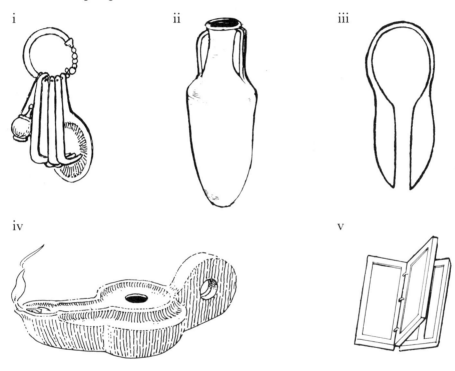

15a How can you tell that the two young men in the foreground of the picture right are not slaves?

15b How could you tell from a man's name that he was not a slave?

15c Explain how a slave's name changed when he was freed.

15d What was one limitation on the rights of a freed slave?

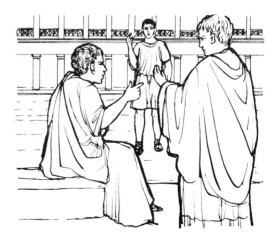

35 points for Part B

NOMEN ....

PART A Understanding the story

Answer all questions on these sheets.
Answer in complete English sentences (unless otherwise instructed).

1 _____ ☐1

2   i   _____
    ii _____
    iii _____
    iv _____
    v   _____
    vi _____ ☐6

3 _____ ☐1

4   i   _____
    ii _____ ☐2

5 _____
  _____ ☐1

6 _____ ☐2

7a _____ ☐1

7b _____ ☐1

8   i   _____   iii _____
    ii _____   iv _____ ☐4

9 _____
  _____
  _____
  _____ ☐3

10 _____ ☐1

30   North American Cambridge Latin Examination: Unit 1 (Form C)

© SCAA Enterprises Limited 1995

NOMEN ....

11 _____ ☐ 1

12 _____
_____
_____ ☐ 1

13 _____
_____
_____ ☐ 2

14 i _____ iii _____
ii _____ iv _____ ☐ 4

15 i _____ iii _____
ii _____ iv _____ ☐ 4

/35 points for Part A

NOMEN ....

PART B Understanding the background

Answer all questions on these sheets.
Answer in complete English sentences (unless otherwise instructed).

1 _____
  _____
  _____ ☐ 3

2 _____
  _____ ☐ 1

3 _____
  _____ ☐ 1

4 _____
  _____
  _____ ☐ 2

5a _____ ☐ 1

5b _____
   _____ ☐ 1

6 _____ ☐ 1

7 _____
  _____
  _____ ☐ 2

8 _____ ☐ 1

9 _____ ☐ 1

10 i _____ ii _____ ☐ 2

11a i _____ ii _____ ☐ 2

11b _____
    _____ ☐ 1

North American Cambridge Latin Examination: Unit 1 (Form C)

© SCAA Enterprises Limited 1995

| NOMEN | .... |

11c _____ ☐1

12 i _____
       ii _____ ☐2

13 _____
       _____
       _____
       _____
       _____ ☐3

14 i   _____
       ii _____
       iii _____
       iv _____
       v   _____ ☐5

15a _____ ☐1

15b _____ ☐1

15c _____
        _____ ☐2

15d _____ ☐1

/35 **points for Part B**

/35 +   /35 =   /70 **points total**

Answer Key

Each question is worth 1 point unless otherwise indicated.

PART A Understanding the story

1. All the Pompeians are on holiday.
2. i Bankers are not banking. / The banker doesn't open his banker's stall.
   ii Judges are not sitting in the lawcourt.
   iii Slaves are not buying food for their masters.
   iv Bakers are not selling bread.
   v Barbers are not trimming beards.
   vi The citizens are not visiting the baths. (6 points total)
3. Messengers are announcing the show.
4. i *audacissimos* (line 7)   ii *feroces* (line 7) (2 points total)
5. Metella, Caecilius, and Quintus are heading for the amphitheater.
6. "What did you do yesterday?" (1) asks Grumio (1). (2 points total)
7a. Clemens was at the theater the day before.
7b. His girlfriend was with him.
8. The main characters were i) a slave, ii) a young man, iii) an old man, and iv) his beautiful daughter. (4 points total)
9. The sequence of action was (3 points in correct sequence):
   i a slave deceived an old man (conspired with a young man to get an old man's money),
   ii a young man caught sight of the old man's beautiful daughter, and/or
   iii fell in love with her instantly,
   iv and the young man gave the money back to the old man. (any three details at 1 point each)
10. Grumio still wonders who went to the theater with Clemens. ("Who went with you to the theater?")
11. Grumio calls Clemens a liar because he believes that Poppaea is his (Grumio's) girlfriend, not Clemens'.
12. Poppaea jilted Grumio for Clemens because she was impressed by Clemens' show of strength when he rescued Caecilius (during an election campaign) from an election riot between rival supporters OR because Clemens had money to spend from Caecilius' reward for saving him during the riot.
13. Any two details from the story for 2 points: Grumio, who was a slave, pretended to be a citizen supporting the bakers' candidate, named Afer. He took "Lucius Spurius Pomponianus" as his alias. As a pseudo-citizen, Grumio accepted bribe money of five denarii from Afer's agent but was then beaten up as a pseudo-citizen by the supporters of Holconius and had his money stolen. (2 points)
14. i *audacissimos* (line 7)   ii *dominis* (line 3)
    iii any one: *decipiebat* (line 12); *cupiebant* (line 13); *erat* (line 13); *habebat* (line 14); *erant* (line 15)
    iv any one: *fecisti* (line 10); *vidimus* (line 11); *spectavimus* (line 12); *conspexit* (line 14); *amavit* (line 15); *reddidit* (line 15); *iit* (line 16); *spectavit* (line 17); *servavi* (line 22). (4 points total)
15. i *spectavimus* (line 12); *conspexit* (line 14); *spectavit* (line 17)
    ii any one: *senem* (line 12); *senex* (line 13); *seni* (line 15)
    iii *exclamat* (line 19)   iv *pulchram* (line 13)

35 points for Part A

PART B Understanding the background

1. Any three: dispersal of information / worship / business / government / socializing.   (3 points)
2. Pompeians would have found written advertisements on walls or on the notice boards (bulletin boards) in the forum.
3. Citizens could go to the baths where they might wrestle, play ball, chat, etc. OR At a dinner party, entertainment might include dancing girls, dwarfs, acrobats, literary recitations, musicians, etc.
4. Any two: An ordinary citizen would have taken along a cushion because the seats were hard stone. He or she would have taken along his or her own refreshments (food, drinks). He or she might have worn a sunhat to protect him or her from the hot Mediterranean sun.   (2 points)
5a. The pictures show theater tickets (tokens).
5b. Important citizens for whom places were reserved would have used them to show the proper entrance and seat number.
6. Five thousand spectators could be seated in the large theater at Pompeii.
7. Any two details: A pantomime was a combination of opera and ballet. The plot was taken from Greek myths. One masked performer danced all the parts and a chorus sang. There was instrumental accompaniment.   (2 points)
8. One famous Roman author of comedies was Plautus / Terence.
9. The presenter of the games might have provided awnings.
10.
    i *retiarius* (netman)
    ii *murmillo* (heavily armed gladiator distinguished by the image of a fish on his helmet)
    (2 points total)
11a. Any two: Jupiter, Apollo, Venus   (2 points)
11b. They worshiped at the *lararium* (household shrine to the *lares*) located usually in the *atrium* or *peristylium*.
11c. Isis
12. Any two: The rooms which might have opened onto the *peristylium* were: the *triclinium* (summer dining room), the *culina* (the kitchen), the slaves' rooms (quarters), the *latrina* (latrine).   (2 points)
13. Any three special features: The garden had a colonnaded walkway (*peristylium*/peristyle) around three or four sides. / The garden had water fountains. / The garden had statues. / The garden might have had a fishpond. / The garden had shrubs and flowers. / The garden, surrounded by a peristyle (enclosed by the house), provided privacy and isolation from the noise on the street.   (3 points)
14.
    i   Strigils and oil pot were used instead of soap in the baths.
    ii Amphora (big jar) was used for storing wine, olive oil, or grain.
    iii The barber's shears (scissors) were used for trimming beards.
    iv An oil lamp was used for lighting since there was no electricity.
    v   A wax tablet was used for writing (homework, letters, accounts, etc.).   (5 points total)
15a. They are wearing togas (which slaves were not allowed to wear).
15b. A citizen had three names. / A slave had only one name.
15c. The slave kept his old name as his last name (1). He added his master's first two names in front of that last name (1).   (2 points total)
15d. Any one: He could not run for public office. / He could not become a (high-ranking) army officer. / He became a client of his former master.

35 points for Part B
Total: 70 points

PART A **Understanding the story**

Read the following story, and then answer the questions based on it.
Answer all questions on the Answer Sheets provided.

candidātus optimus

Grumiō in culīnā sedēbat. īrātus erat quod mercātōrēs eum in forō
verberāvērunt. īrātus quoque erat quod mercātōrēs dēnāriōs suōs
rapuērunt.
    Metella culīnam intrāvit.
    "Grumiō, cūr tū togam geris?" rogāvit Metella. "quid tū fēcistī?" 5
servus Metellae tōtam rem nārrāvit.
    "tūne Afrō favēs?" inquit Metella. "sed tū es stultus, quod Āfer est
caudex. Marcus Fūfidius Pulcher est candidātus optimus. ego et
Quīntus Fūfidiō favēmus quod āthlēta nōtissimus est. Caecilius quoque
est asinus quod Holcōniō favet. ego cōnsilium optimum habeō." 10
    postquam nox vēnit, Grumiō cum Sullā in viā stābat.
    Grumiō scrīptōrī dīxit, "tacē, Sulla! Caecilius in vīllā dormit. nunc
scrībe hunc titulum in mūrō: 'Fūfidius est candidātus optimus.
Caecilius Fūfidiō favet.' "
    Grumiō, postquam Sulla titulum scrīpsit, vehementer exclāmāvit. 15
    "euge! hic titulus mē valdē dēlectat!"
    Caecilius tamen clāmōrem audīvit et ē vīllā festīnāvit.
    "cūr vōs clāmōrem facitis? cūr nōn dormītis?" clāmāvit. tum titulum
lēgit. quod īrātissimus erat, Grumiōnem et Sullam vituperāvit.
    Metella et Quīntus quoque ē vīllā celeriter discessērunt. 20
    "tacē, Caecilī!" clāmāvit Metella. "Sulla titulum scrīpsit quod ego
Sullae decem dēnāriōs dedī."
    "Metella," Caecilius uxōrī respondit, "es stultissima, quod candidātō
meō nōn favēs."
    "pater," inquit Quīntus, "hic titulus mihi placet. ego Fūfidiō faveō, 25
et ego quoque sum Caecilius."

dēnārius	*denarius, coin*
gerit	*is wearing*
cōnsilium	*plan, idea*
nox: noctem	*night*
titulus	*slogan*
dēlectat	*pleases*
discēdit	*departs, leaves:* discessit

PART A **Understanding the story**

Answer all questions on the Answer Sheets provided.
Answer in complete English sentences (unless otherwise instructed).

1   Where was Grumio at the beginning of the story?

2   *īrātus erat* (line 2): give two reasons why Grumio felt this way.

3   Metella noticed that something was wrong.
   i   What was wrong?
   ii Why was it wrong?

4   In other stories which you have read in class, what other thing had Grumio done that was, in fact, illegal?

5a Write the **Latin** word that Metella used to express her opinion of Grumio.

5b Why did Metella describe Grumio in this way?

6a List the names of the persons who supported Marcus Fufidius Pulcher in the election.

6b Write a **Latin** phrase that shows why Fufidius had their support.

7   Why did Metella refer to Caecilius as *asinus*?

8   What was Sulla's occupation?

9a Why did Grumio say, *"tacē, Sulla!"*? (line 12)

9b Then what did Grumio ask Sulla to do?

10 Why would you expect Caecilius to be angry at the words: *"Fūfidius est candidātus optimus. Caecilius Fūfidiō favet."*? (lines 13–14)

11 What **Latin** words show Grumio's opinion of Sulla's work?

12a How did Grumio cause trouble for himself when he said these words?

12b What was one result of Grumio's blunder?

13 Translate into English *"cūr vōs clāmōrem facitis? cūr nōn dormītis?"* (line 18)

14 What two things did Caecilius do after he asked his questions?

15 Write the **Latin** word that shows that Metella did not share Caecilius' opinion.

16 What part did Metella admit she had played in Sulla's assignment?

17 Translate into English: *"es stultissima, quod candidātō meō nōn favēs."* (lines 23–24)

18 How did Quintus justify the wording of the slogan?

North American Cambridge Latin Examination: Unit 1 (Form D)

© SCAA Enterprises Limited 1995

19 From the story find an example of each of the following:
  i a verb in the imperfect tense
  ii a plural noun in the accusative case

20 Which **Latin** words in the story provide the roots for the following English words?
  i audition
  ii illegible
  iii reverberate
  iv sedentary

35 points for Part A

PART B Understanding the background

Answer all questions on the Answer Sheets provided.
Answer in complete English sentences (unless otherwise instructed).

1a What event is illustrated by the picture on the right?

1b Why might the bakers be supporting Rufus?

1c What was the main job of a *duovir*?

2 Election slogans were painted on the walls of buildings in Pompeii.

2a "The barbers recommend Trebius for aedile."
What were **two** of the duties of an aedile?

2b "All the people who are fast asleep vote for Vatia."
What is one thing which this slogan tells you about Pompeian election campaigns?

2c "We want Titus Claudius Verus for duovir."
What does this candidate's name tell you about his social status?

3 Study the map of Pompeii on your Answer Sheet. In six of the squares on your Answer Sheet, locate and label the following items:

A B C

North American Cambridge Latin Examination: Unit 1 (Form D)

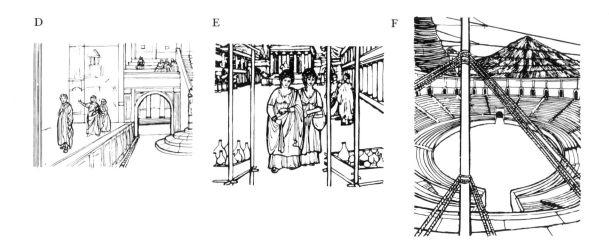

4a Examine this picture. How did the Pompeians get clean in this room? Mention **two** details.

4b What is the **Latin** name for this room?

5 Examine this picture. On your Answer Sheet, label the *impluvium* and the *lararium*.

6 State **two** reasons why there was a hole in the ceiling of this room.

7   State **two** disadvantages of being a slave.

8   State **two** reasons why a slave might have been set free.

9   State **one** reason why the slave might have preferred to remain a slave.

10 Name **two** types of performance which might have been presented here.

11 Why have the women probably come to this part of Pompeii?

12 Name **three other** activities which took place in this location.

13 Name one event that usually took place in this location.

14 What item shown in this picture has been provided for the comfort of some of the spectators?

15a Who normally paid the expenses in order to stage the events here?

15b Why would this person pay these expenses?

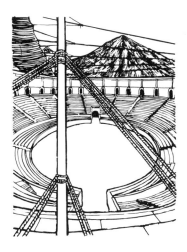

35 points for Part B

NOMEN ....

PART A   Understanding the story

Answer all questions on these sheets.
Answer in complete English sentences (unless otherwise instructed).

1 _____ ☐1

2   i _____
    ii _____ ☐2

3   i _____ ☐1
    ii _____ ☐1

4   _____
    _____
    _____ ☐1

5a Latin word: _____ ☐1

5b _____
    _____
    _____ ☐2

6a i _____
    ii _____ ☐2

6b Latin phrase: _____ ☐1

7   _____ ☐1

8   _____ ☐1

9a _____ ☐1

9b _____ ☐1

10 _____ ☐1

11 Latin words: _____ ☐1

12a _____ ☐1

North American Cambridge Latin Examination: Unit 1 (Form D)

© SCAA Enterprises Limited 1995

NOMEN ....

12b _____ ☐1

13 _____
_____
_____ ☐2

14 i _____
ii _____ ☐2

15 Latin word: _____ ☐1

16 _____ ☐1

17 _____
_____ ☐2

18 _____ ☐1

19 i _____ ☐1
ii _____ ☐1

20 i _____ ☐1
ii _____ ☐1
iii _____ ☐1
iv _____ ☐1

/35 **points for Part A**

North American Cambridge Latin Examination: Unit 1 (Form D)

© SCAA Enterprises Limited 1995

NOMEN ....

PART B Understanding the background

Answer all questions on these sheets.
Answer in complete English sentences (unless otherwise instructed).

1a _____ ☐ 1

1b _____ ☐ 1

1c _____ ☐ 1

2a i _____

   ii _____
   _____ ☐ 2

2b _____ ☐ 1

2c _____ ☐ 1

3

☐ 6

4a i _____
   ii _____ ☐ 2

4b Latin name: _____ ☐ 1

44   North American Cambridge Latin Examination: Unit 1 (Form D)

© SCAA Enterprises Limited 1995

NOMEN ....

5

☐ 2

6   i   _____
       ii   _____ ☐ 2

7   i   _____
       ii   _____ ☐ 2

8   i   _____
       ii   _____ ☐ 2

9   _____ ☐ 1

10   i   _____ ii   _____ ☐ 2

11   _____ ☐ 1

12   i   _____
       ii   _____
       iii   _____ ☐ 3

13   _____ ☐ 1

14   _____ ☐ 1

15a   _____ ☐ 1

15b   _____ ☐ 1

/35 points for Part B

/35 +   /35 =   /70 points total

North American Cambridge Latin Examination: Unit 1 (Form D)

Answer Key

Each question is worth 1 point unless otherwise indicated.

PART A Understanding the story

1 Grumio was in the kitchen.

2 i The merchants beat him up in the forum.
ii The merchants seized/stole his money/denarii.   (2 points total)

3 i Grumio was wearing a toga.
ii Grumio was a slave and not permitted by law to wear a toga.   (2 points total)

4 One of: Grumio masqueraded as Lucius Spurius Pomponianus, a citizen and a baker. Grumio accepted an election bribe as a voter.

5a *stultus*

5b Any two of: Grumio supported Afer, and Metella said that Afer was a blockhead (*caudex*). Metella supported Fufidius/Marcus Fufidius Pulcher.   (2 points)

6a i Quintus
ii Metella   (2 points total)

6b *est candidatus optimus / est athleta notissimus*

7 Caecilius supported Holconius.

8 Sulla was a sign-writer/*scriptor*.

9a Grumio told Sulla to be quiet because Caecilius was sleeping in the house.

9b Grumio told Sulla to write an election slogan on the wall.

10 Caecilius supported Holconius, not Fufidius.

11 *euge! / hic titulus me valde delectat!*

12a Grumio yelled.

12b Any one of: Caecilius heard the shouting. Caecilius hurried out of the house.

13 "Why are you making an uproar/noise? (1) Why are you not sleeping/asleep? (1)"   (2 points total)

14 i Caecilius read the slogan.
ii Caecilius cursed Grumio and Sulla.   (2 points total)

15 *tace*

16 Metella gave Sulla ten denarii. OR Metella planned the whole operation.

17 "You are very stupid (1), because you do not support my candidate. (1)"   (2 points total)

18 Quintus said that his name was Caecilius, too.

19 i *sedebat* (line 1) / *erat* (lines 1, 2 & 19) / *stabat* (line 11)
ii *denarios* (line 22)

20 i *audivit* (line 17)
ii *legit* (line 19)
iii *verberaverunt* (line 2)
iv *sedebat* (line 1)

35 points for Part A

PART B Understanding the background

1a The picture illustrates an election speech/rally/campaign.

1b Often a candidate was nominated/supported by a particular trade group. OR Rufus was probably a baker, too.

1c A duovir heard evidence and gave judgment in the law court/*basilica*.

2a Any two: An aedile supervised public markets, police force, baths, places of entertainment, water supply, sewers. An aedile oversaw the operation of an efficient public service, spending of tax money.   (2 points)

2b Any one: Citizens could and did ridicule electoral candidates. There was some degree of free speech. Voters were literate.

2c He was a citizen.

3

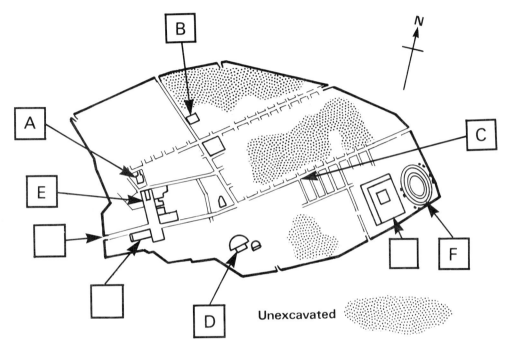

(6 points)

4a Any two: The Pompeians would soak in the hot pool, massage oil into the skin, scrape off oil and impurities with strigils.   (2 points)

4b *caldarium*

5

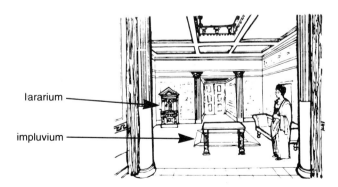

(2 points)

North American Cambridge Latin Examination: Unit 1 (Form D)

6	Any two: The hole in the ceiling let in light, provided a source of moving air in hot weather, admitted rainwater for the impluvium, let out smoke and fumes, was traditional / houses always had one. (2 points)
7	Any two: Slaves were treated as property by law, had no control of their own lives, could not enter into marriages recognized by law, were often treated harshly, suffered harsh punishments, worked long hours, had poor living conditions, were entitled to little legal protection, were frequently separated from friends, family, native land, culture, language. (2 points)
8	Any two: A slave might be freed in his master's will. A slave might be rewarded for good service by being freed. A slave might be freed as a sign of friendship and respect. A slave might buy his freedom (with his *peculium*, the money allowance which a slave could put aside towards the purchase of his own freedom). (2 points)
9	Any one: The master provided food and a place to live. A slave might have had no training in directing his own affairs. A slave would have no guarantee of finding employment. The slave might have enjoyed his work. The living quarters as a slave might have been better than any available to him as a freedman. He might have had a good master who treated him well.
10	Any two: Comedy, tragedy, pantomime, farces, musical concerts were performed here. (2 points)
11	The women probably came to shop.
12	Any three: The forum was a center for dispersal of information, worship, for business, for government, for administration of justice, for socializing. [N.B. If the student has incorrectly identified the location in question 11, allow answers which are consistent with the location she/he has selected.] (3 points)
13	Any one: Gladiatorial fights and beast hunts took place here.
14	An awning was provided for the comfort of the spectators.
15a	An electoral candidate / wealthy citizen paid the expenses.
15b	He did so to gain popularity.

35 points for Part B
Total: 70 points

PART A Understanding the story

Read the following story, and then answer the questions based on it.
Answer all questions on the Answer Sheets provided.

fūrēs

Metella et Melissa ē forō reveniēbant. Metella Caeciliō <u>dōnum</u>
portābat, quod Caecilius diem nātālem celebrābat. dōnum erat ānulus.
Grumiō Caeciliō cēnam splendidam parābat.

    Metella, postquam ātrium intrāvit, Quīntum et Grumiōnem vocāvit.
<u>nēmō</u> respondit. Cerberus nōn <u>lātrāvit</u>.   5

    "Melissa, Grumiōnem in culīnā quaere!" inquit Metella.

    Metella Quīntum in triclīniō, in tablīnō, in hortō quaesīvit. fēminae,
quod <u>nēminem</u> invēnērunt, erant sollicitae.

    "Grumiōne cibum in forō emit?" rogāvit Melissa.

    "minimē! multum cibum in culīnā habet," respondit Metella.   10

    "num Quīntus amīcōs cum Cerberō vīsitat?" inquit Melissa.

    "minimē!" respondit Metella. "Cerberus vīllam semper custōdit."

    ad ātrium revēnērunt Metella et ancilla. tum <u>arcam</u> <u>apertam</u>
cōnspexērunt. Caecilius pecūniam in arcā habēbat. Metella et Melissa
erant sollicitiōrēs. arcam īnspexērunt. pecūnia aberat! subitō <u>sonum</u> in   15
cubiculō audīvērunt. fēminae erant perterritae. tacitē sed fortiter ad
cubiculum festīnāvērunt. <u>ibi</u> Quīntus ē <u>lectō</u> <u>lentē</u> surgēbat, sed
Grumiō et Cerberus in terrā <u>exanimātī</u> iacēbant.

    "duo fūrēs nōs pulsāvērunt et superāvērunt," <u>susurrāvit</u> Quīntus.
"ego tamen fūrēs agnōvī. fūrēs erant Hermogenēs et Anthrāx."   20

    mox Caecilius vīllam intrāvit. Metella tōtam rem nārrāvit. Caecilius
erat īrātissimus.

    "nēmō est <u>scelestior</u> quam Hermogenēs," exclāmāvit. "ōlim
Hermogenēs mihi pecūniam nōn reddidit."

    Caecilius, postquam omnēs <u>adiūvit</u>, ad basilicam contendit. (<u>posteā</u>   25
iūdex Hermogenem et Anthrācem ibi <u>convīcit</u>.) dominus tamen, quod
fūrēs pecūniam cēpērunt et filium et servum verberāvērunt, diem
nātālem <u>postrīdiē</u> celebrāvit, et ānulum laetus accēpit.

dōnum	*gift, present*	lentē	*slowly*
nēmō: nēminem	*nobody*	exanimātus	*unconscious*
lātrat	*barks*	susurrat	*whispers*: susurrāvit
arca: arcam	*chest, strongbox*	scelestior	*more wicked, more evil*
apertus	*open*	adiuvat	*helps*: adiūvit
sonus	*sound*	posteā	*afterwards, later*
ibi	*there*	convincit	*convicts*: convīcit
lectus	*bed, couch*	postrīdiē	*the next day*

PART A   Understanding the story

Answer all questions on the Answer Sheets provided.
Answer in complete English sentences (unless otherwise instructed).

1 What gift did Metella buy in the forum?

2 For whom was this purchase made?

3 What was the reason for the purchase?

4 What was Grumio doing during the absence of Metella and Melissa?

5 Which persons was Metella expecting to find in the house?

6 Which areas did Metella enter in her search for the persons she expected to see at home? (Use English names for these areas.)

7 Translate into English: *fēminae, quod nēminem invēnērunt, erant sollicitae.* (lines 7–8)

8 Why was Metella suspicious about the absence of one of the household members? (line 10)

9 Translate into English: *num Quīntus amīcōs cum Cerberō vīsitat?* (line 11)

10 Give two **Latin adjectives** which describe the feelings of Metella and Melissa when they were back in the atrium.

11 For each adjective, explain why they felt this way.

12 Where did they go after returning to the atrium?

13 Explain why they went there.

14 What was Quintus doing there?

15 What was the condition of Cerberus?

16a What were the two pieces of information that Metella and Melissa received from Quintus?

16b How did Caecilius find out the information?

17 Give the **Latin** word that describes Caecilius' reaction upon hearing what had happened.

18 Where did Caecilius go after hearing Metella's story?

19 What happened to Hermogenes and Anthrax?

20 What was one enjoyable thing that happened to Caecilius on his birthday?

21 From the story, select one example of each of the following:
   i   a verb that is in the imperfect tense
   ii a noun that is accusative plural
   iii an adjective that is in the comparative degree

22 Which **Latin words** in the passage give the following English derivatives?
  i invention
  ii insurgent
  iii adjacent

35 points for Part A

PART B # Understanding the background

Answer all questions on the Answer Sheets provided.
Answer in complete English sentences (unless otherwise instructed).

1. On the plan of Pompeii on your Answer Sheet, label the places marked by arrows.

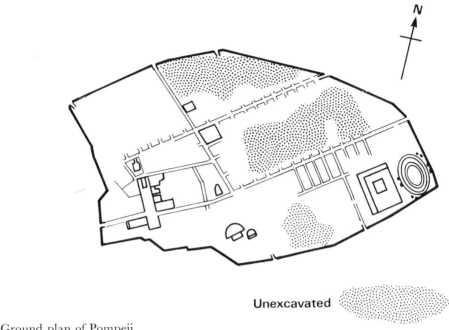

Ground plan of Pompeii

Unexcavated

A: Caecilius' house
B: the place where you would see a *fābula*
C: the area where the speakers' platform was located
D: the building where a *tepidārium* would be found
E: the place where you would watch a *spectāculum*

2. A *cēna* in Caecilius' house is mentioned in the story. Give the following information about a typical *cēna*:
   i the time of day when it was held
   ii one type of appetizer served
   iii the dessert offered

3 In the diagram of the house on your Answer Sheet, label the following items:

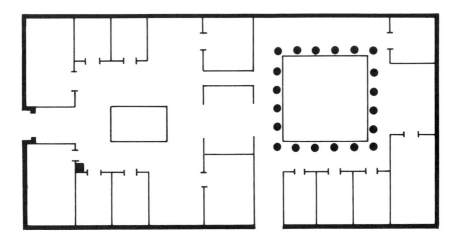

A: *peristȳlium*
B: *tablīnum*
C: *larārium*
D: *triclīnium*
E: *impluvium*

4 A Roman household depended on slavery for its efficient operation, as we have seen in Caecilius' house.

4a Give two ways in which people became slaves.

4b What did "manumission" mean, to a slave?

5 While Pompeians might have seen a *fābula* in the area you were asked to identify in question 1, they would often have **read** or **heard** a *fābula* at school. Identify the following authors by putting the correct letter beside the appropriate description on your Answer Sheet:

A: Plautus
B: Aeschylus
C: Homer
D: Vergil

6 Answer the following questions, also related to Roman schooling:
  i From what two materials was a *tabula* made?
  ii What was the purpose of a *stilus*?
  iii What was a *ludī magister*?

7   A Roman *cēna* was often preceded by a visit to the kind of building represented in the diagram on your Answer Sheet. On the diagram, label the places marked by arrows:

A: *palaestra*
B: *caldārium*
C: *frigidārium*
D: *apodytērium*

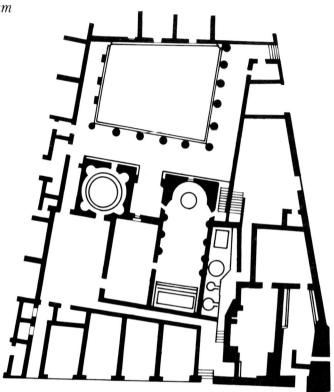

8   Attending a *spectāculum* was another leisure-time pursuit. At this event, you might see each of the following men. On your Answer Sheet correctly identify them by placing the appropriate letter below each picture.

A: *rētiārius*
B: *murmillō*
C: *bēstiārius*

9 The events in which each of these men took part originally provided entertainment at Roman funerals. After a Pompeian's death, relatives would often place offerings at his/her tomb. Indicate three types of offering that might have been placed there.

10 At the speaker's platform, you might hear a *candidātus* who was campaigning for the office of *duovir*.

10a Give the origin of the word *candidātus*.

10b What was one duty of a *duovir*?

35 points for Part B

NOMEN ....

PART A Understanding the story

Answer all questions on these sheets.
Answer in complete English sentences (unless otherwise instructed).

1 _____ ☐1

2 _____ ☐1

3 _____ ☐1

4 _____ ☐1

5 _____ ☐2

6   i _____

    ii _____

    iii _____ ☐3

7 _____
_____ ☐2

8 _____
_____ ☐1

9 _____
_____ ☐2

10 Latin adjectives: i _____

                      ii _____ ☐2

11 i _____
_____

    ii _____
_____ ☐2

12 _____ ☐1

13 _____ ☐1

14 _____ ☐1

North American Cambridge Latin Examination: Unit 1 (Form E)

© SCAA Enterprises Limited 1995

NOMEN ....

15 _____ ☐1

16a i _____
     ii _____ ☐2

16b _____ ☐1

17 Latin word: _____ ☐1

18 _____ ☐1

19 _____ ☐1

20 _____ ☐1

21 i _____ ☐1
    ii _____ ☐1
    iii _____ ☐1

22 i _____ ☐1
    ii _____ ☐1
    iii _____ ☐1

/35 points for Part A

NOMEN ....

PART B Understanding the background

Answer all questions on these sheets.
Answer in complete English sentences (unless otherwise instructed).

1

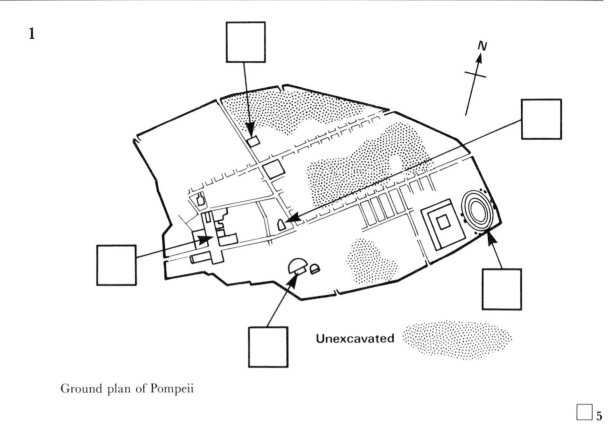

Ground plan of Pompeii

☐ 5

2 i _____ ☐ 1
   ii _____ ☐ 1
   iii _____ ☐ 1

NOMEN ....

3

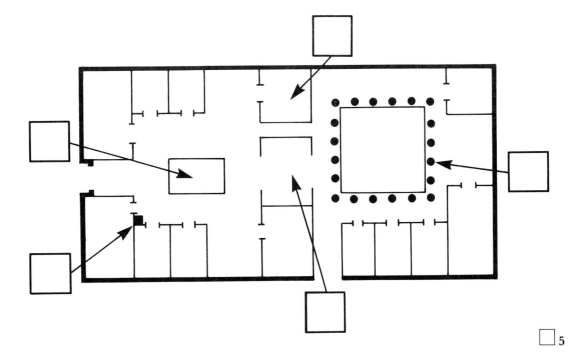

☐ 5

4a i _____
ii _____ ☐ 2

4b _____ ☐ 1

5 a Greek writer of tragedies _____
the author of the *Iliad* _____
a Roman writer of comedies _____
the author of the *Aeneid* _____ ☐ 4

6 i _____ ☐ 1
ii _____ ☐ 1
iii _____ ☐ 1

NOMEN ....

7

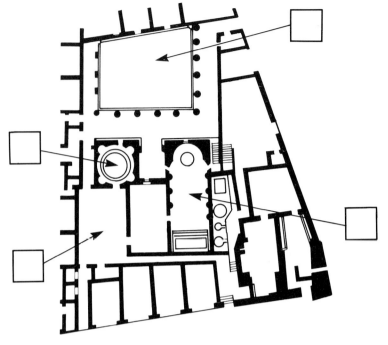

☐4

8

_____   _____   _____

☐3

9 i _____
    ii _____
    iii _____   ☐3

10a _____
      _____ ☐1

10b _____ ☐1

/35 points for Part B

/35 +   /35 =   /70 points total

Answer Key

Each question is worth 1 point unless otherwise indicated.

PART A Understanding the story

1. Metella bought a ring.
2. The purchase was made for Caecilius.
3. Caecilius was celebrating his birthday.
4. Grumio was preparing a splendid dinner for Caecilius.
5. Metella was expecting to find Quintus and Grumio in the house. (2 points)
6. She entered the dining room, study, and garden. (3 points total)
7. The women were worried (1), because they found nobody (1). (2 points total)
8. Grumio had no need to leave the house to buy food, because he had a lot of food in the kitchen.
9. "Surely Quintus is not visiting (1) friends with Cerberus? (1)" (2 points total)
10. i *sollicitiores*
    ii *perterritae* (2 points)
11. i They were (more) worried because the chest was open / Caecilius kept his money there.
    ii They were frightened because they heard a noise. (2 points)
12. They went to the bedroom.
13. They went there because they heard a noise.
14. Quintus was getting up (slowly) from the bed.
15. Cerberus was unconscious.
16a. Any two: Quintus told Metella and Melissa that they had been beaten and overpowered by two thieves, that he had recognized the thieves, and that they were Hermogenes and Anthrax. (2 points)
16b. Metella told him.
17. *iratissimus*
18. Caecilius went to the lawcourt (basilica).
19. Hermogenes and Anthrax were convicted by the judge.
20. He received his present / the ring.
21. i many examples
    ii *amicos* (line 11); *fures* (line 20); *omnes* (line 25)
    iii *sollicitiores* (line 15); *scelestior* (line 23)
22. i *invenerunt* (line 8)
    ii *surgebat* (line 17)
    iii *iacebant* (line 18)

35 points for Part A

PART B Understanding the background

1. Clockwise from the bottom left-hand corner: C, A, D, E, B (5 points)
2. i It was held toward the end of the afternoon.
   ii Eggs/fish would be served.
   iii Fruit and cheese would be offered.
3. Clockwise from the bottom left-hand corner: C, E, D, A, B (5 points)

4a Any two: People became slaves through being prisoners of war or through being captured by pirates, or through being born into slavery. (2 points)

4b "Manumission" was the act of setting a slave free.

5 B, C, A, D (4 points)

6
  i A *tabula* was made from wood and wax.
  ii A *stilus* was used for inscribing on and/or erasing from the *tabula*.
  iii The *ludi magister* was the teacher of the first school attended by Roman children.

7 Clockwise from the bottom left-hand corner: D, C, A, B (4 points)

8 From left to right: B, C, A (3 points)

9 Any three: Flowers, eggs, beans, lentils, flour, wine, and blood might have been placed as offerings on a tomb. (3 points)

10a The word *candidatus* is derived from the Latin word for "white/dazzling" (*candidus*): a candidate was dressed in a specially whitened toga.

10b The *duoviri* had the responsibility for hearing court cases and passing judgment on these.

35 points for Part B
Total: 70 points

PART A Understanding the story

Read the following story, and then answer the questions based on it.
Answer all questions on the Answer Sheets provided.

Grumiō diem malum agit

hodiē Grumiō sērō surgit. coquus dolet. corpus dolet quod heri
mercātōrēs in forō eum verberāvērunt et caput dolet quod nimium vīnī
in culīnā postrēmā nocte bibit. Grumiō īrātus erat quod Clēmēns
Poppaeam vīsitābat.

Clēmēns tamen, postquam ad vīllam revēnit, nūntiāvit, "ī ad   5
cubiculum tuum, Grumiō, et dormī! ego Poppaeae nōn placeō.
Poppaea tē valdē amat."

nunc Grumiō tunicam quam celerrimē induit. dominō et familiae
ientāculum dat.

Caecilius nōn laetus est, quod ientāculum sērum est; Grumiōnem   10
igitur vituperat. Melissa tacitē lacrimat quod Grumiō hodiē diem
nātālem celebrat sed nēmō scit.

post ientāculum Grumiō ad forum ambulat. coquus in forō multās
tabernās intrat, ubi cibum quaerit. tandem pāvōnem vīvum emit. mox
coquus vīllam cum pāvōne intrat.   15

ēheu! pāvō ā Grumiōne effugit et in Metellam salit. Grumiō clāmat
et pāvō tablīnum intrat. pāvō nunc in mēnsā stat ubi cērae sunt.
Caecilius est īrātissimus. pāvō tum in peristȳlium volat. Cerberus
pāvōnem in hortō videt et lātrat. pāvō nunc in triclīnium volat ubi
Quīntus in lectō recumbit et vīnum ē pōculō bibit. Quīntus subitō   20
surgit et vīnum effundit. tandem pāvō in culīnam volat et Grumiō
nunc cēnam coquit.

post cēnam Caecilius Grumiōnem in triclīnium vocat. Grumiō est
sollicitus. Caecilius inquit, "nōs omnēs diem malum aliquandō
agimus." tum dominus Grumiōnī dōnum dat et omnēs hospitēs   25
clāmant, "fēlīcem diem nātālem, Grumiō!" Grumiō valdē rīdet.

diem . . . agit	has a day, experiences a day	sērum	late
malus	bad	nēmō	no one
sērō	too late	scit	knows
dolet	hurts	pāvō: pāvōnem	peacock
corpus	body	vīvus	live, living
caput	head	effugit	escapes
nimium vīnī	too much wine	salit	jumps
postrēmā nocte	last night	volat	flies
ī	go!	lātrat	barks
amat	loves	lectus	couch
quam celerrimē	as quickly as possible	effundit	spills
induit	puts on	aliquandō	now and then
ientāculum	breakfast	dōnum	gift
		fēlīx: fēlīcem	happy

© SCAA Enterprises Limited 1995

PART A Understanding the story

Answer all questions on the Answer Sheets provided.
Answer in complete English sentences (unless otherwise instructed).

1. At the beginning of the story, how is Grumio's behavior affected by the fact that he is in pain?

2. What two specific reasons for his pain are mentioned in lines 1–3?

3. From your memory of the stories in Unit 1, briefly summarize the incident that led to the events mentioned in lines 1–4.

4. Why should Grumio feel relieved after hearing what Clemens has said?

5. Why does Caecilius scold Grumio in lines 10–11?

6. On your Answer Sheet circle the letter of the word that best describes Melissa's attitude toward Grumio in line 11:

   A   indifferent   B   impatient   C   sympathetic

7. Based on the stories in Unit 1, explain why you would or would not expect this attitude from Melissa.

8. What does Grumio do in the forum?

9. In which room is Metella, probably, when the events in line 16 take place?

10. Who is the next "victim"?

11. Write the **Latin** word that shows the mood or the reaction of the "victim" in question 10.

12. What area of the house is next affected? (line 18)

13. Which member of the household is affected in that area?

14. How does the "visitor" affect Quintus?

15. In what room does the "visitor" finally end his tour?

16. Explain why this is good or bad for Grumio.

17. When does Caecilius call for Grumio?

18. How does Grumio feel when this happens?

19. Suggest why he would feel this way.

20. Translate Caecilius' reassuring statement to Grumio: "*nōs omnēs diem malum aliquandō agimus.*" (lines 24–25)

21. Give two reasons you learned from the story which prove that Grumio's last twenty-four hours have not been so bad after all.

22 In the story, find an example of each of the following items:
  i   a plural noun in the accusative case
  ii a singular noun in the dative case
  iii a verb in the imperfect tense
  iv a verb in the perfect tense
  v   a superlative adjective

23 List the **Latin** words from the story which provide the root of the following English words:
  i   enunciate
  ii horticulture
  iii innate
  iv ridiculous
  v   tacit

35 points for Part A

PART B Understanding the background

Answer all questions on the Answer Sheets provided.
Answer in complete English sentences (unless otherwise instructed).

1. Study the following pictures. In the blanks on your Answer Sheet write the letter of each picture **in the order** it was visited by Grumio's special guest.

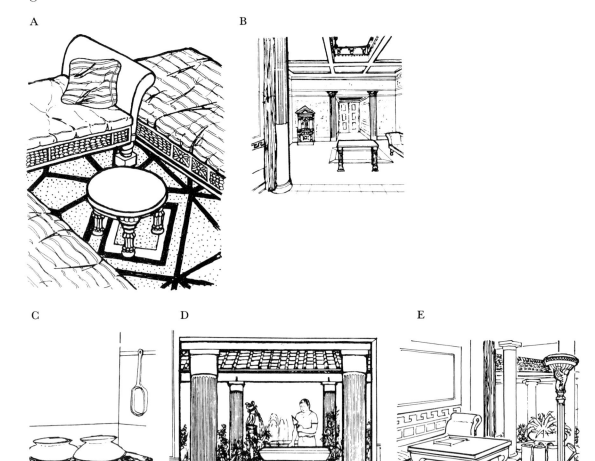

2. What two things would Grumio have served the family for *ientāculum*?
3a. Write the **Latin** word for *dinner*. (It occurred in the story.)
3b. At what time of day was this meal served?
3c. How many courses did it usually have?

4 On your Answer Sheet, write the number for each city as it appears on the map.

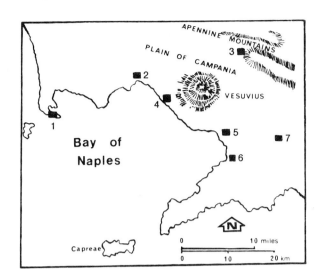

A: Herculaneum
B: Misenum
C: Neapolis
D: Nuceria
E: Pompeii

5a What does the term *manūmissiō* have to do with slavery in the ancient world?

5b Give two details about *manūmissiō*.

6a What was a *lībertus*?

6b What were two restrictions on his life?

7a Why did the Romans bury their dead beside busy roads?

7b Why did the Romans often bring the dead a gift of wine?

7c What did the Greek Epicurus think happened to a person or his soul after he died?

8a Which type of building in Pompeii would make use of a *hypocaust*?

8b Give two details of how a hypocaust worked.

9 What was the function of an *apodytērium*?

10a What two groups were involved in the Great Riot of A.D. 59?

10b What was the penalty Pompeii had to pay after the riot?

11 With what two items of equipment did a *rētiārius* fight?

12 What was a *grammaticus*?

13 If a student used *tabulae*, with what would he write?

14 If a student used a *papyrus*, with what would he write?

35 points for Part B
Total: 70 points

NOMEN ....

PART A Understanding the story

Answer all questions on these sheets.
Answer in complete English sentences (unless otherwise instructed).

1 _____ ☐1

2 i _____
   ii _____ ☐2

3 _____
  _____
  _____ ☐2

4 _____ ☐1

5 _____ ☐1

6 A   B   C   ☐1

7 _____
  _____
  _____ ☐1

8 _____ ☐1

9 _____ ☐1

10 _____ ☐1

11 Latin word: _____ ☐1

12 _____ ☐1

13 _____ ☐1

14 _____ ☐1

15 _____ ☐1

16 _____
                                                                  ☐1

North American Cambridge Latin Examination: Unit 1 (Form F)

© SCAA Enterprises Limited 1995

NOMEN ....

17 _____ ☐ 1

18 _____ ☐ 1

19 _____ ☐ 1

20 _____
   _____ ☐ 2

21 i _____
       _____
    ii _____
       _____ ☐ 2

22 i   _____ ☐ 1
    ii _____ ☐ 1
    iii _____ ☐ 1
    iv _____ ☐ 1
    v   _____ ☐ 1

23 i   _____ ☐ 1
    ii _____ ☐ 1
    iii _____ ☐ 1
    iv _____ ☐ 1
    v   _____ ☐ 1

/35 **points for Part A**

NOMEN ....

PART B **Understanding the background**

Answer all questions on these sheets.
Answer in complete English sentences (unless otherwise instructed).

1

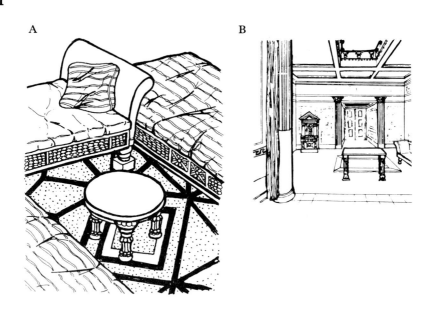

        1st ___ 2nd ___ 3rd ___ 4th ___ 5th ___   ☐5

2   i _____

      ii _____   ☐2

3a Latin word: _____   ☐1

3b _____   ☐1

3c _____   ☐1

NOMEN ....

4 A: Herculaneum _____
   B: Misenum _____
   C: Neapolis _____
   D: Nuceria _____
   E: Pompeii _____

☐ 5

5a _____ ☐ 1

5b i _____
       _____

    ii _____
       _____ ☐ 2

6a _____ ☐ 1

6b i _____
    ii _____ ☐ 2

7a _____
    _____ ☐ 1

7b _____
    _____ ☐ 1

7c _____
    _____ ☐ 1

8a _____ ☐ 1

8b i _____
    ii _____ ☐ 2

9   _____
    _____ ☐ 1

10a _____
    _____ ☐ 1

North American Cambridge Latin Examination: Unit 1 (Form F)

10b _____ □ 1

11 i _____
ii _____ □ 2

12 _____ □ 1

13 _____ □ 1

14 _____ □ 1

/35 **points for Part B**

/35 + /35 = /70 **points total**

Answer Key

Each question is worth 1 point unless otherwise indicated.

PART A   Understanding the story

1. He has woken up too late.
2. Merchants beat him up in the forum the day before, and (his head hurts because) last night he drank too much wine.   (2 points)
3. Any two points: Grumio had impersonated a Roman citizen the day before in the forum, when the Pompeians were listening to political speeches. He was beaten by merchants who supported the opposition candidate. He returned home in a sorry state only to learn that Clemens had a date with Poppaea. [Versions of this story which emphasize different details may be accepted, according to the teacher's discretion.]   (2 points)
4. Grumio still had the loyalty of his girlfriend Poppaea, after all.
5. Caecilius scolds Grumio because breakfast has been served late.
6. C (sympathetic)
7. You *would not* expect this attitude from Melissa, because Grumio scolded Melissa and made her cry on the occasion when she cooked a meal and used up all the supplies in the kitchen, leaving him with none for the next day. OR You *would* expect this attitude from Melissa because she is tender-hearted and tries to help out around the house (cooking, writing, etc.) *or* because Grumio seems to be able to persuade women to like him despite his faults (e.g. Poppaea).
8. Grumio buys a live peacock in the forum.
9. Metella is probably in the atrium (because the peacock flies onto her as soon as Grumio enters the house).
10. Caecilius is the next "victim."
11. *iratissimus*
12. The peristyle (*peristylium*) or garden is affected next.
13. Cerberus is affected in the garden.
14. The peacock makes Quintus rise up suddenly and spill his wine.
15. The peacock ends his tour in the kitchen.
16. It is a good thing for Grumio that the peacock ends up in the kitchen, as he can now get on with the dinner preparations (i.e. cooking the peacock!).
17. Caecilius calls for Grumio after dinner is finished.
18. Grumio feels worried when this happens.
19. Grumio probably expects to be scolded by Caecilius (since things have not gone well up to this point).
20. "We all have (1) a bad day now and then (1)."   (2 points total)
21. Any two:
    i Grumio got to keep his girlfriend after all.   ii Caecilius is not really angry with Grumio.
    iii People did remember Grumio's birthday after all.   (2 points)
22. i *tabernas* (line 14)   ii *Poppaeae* (line 6); *domino* (line 8); *familiae* (line 8); *Grumioni* (line 25)
    iii *erat* (line 3); *visitabat* (line 4)
    iv *verberaverunt* (line 2); *bibit* (line 3); *revenit* (line 5); *nuntiavit* (line 5)   v *iratissimus* (line 18)
23. i *nuntiavit* (line 5)   ii *horto* [*hortus*] (line 19)   iii *natalem* [*natalis*] (lines 12 & 26)
    iv *ridet* (line 26)   v *tacite* (line 11)

35 points for Part A

PART B Understanding the background

1 1st: B   2nd: E   3rd: D   4th: A   5th: C
[Partial credit may be given to students who get some, but not all, of the rooms in the correct order, or to students who have two or three rooms in the right order but not in the right blanks.]   (5 points)

2 i bread   ii water   (2 points)

3a *cena*

3b Dinner was served toward the end of the afternoon.

3c Dinner usually consisted of three courses.

4 A: 4   B: 1   C: 2   D: 7   E: 5   (5 points)

5a *manumissio* was the act of freeing a slave.

5b Any two details: *manumissio* could be a legal ceremony before a judge, in the presence of a witness. The slave's head would be touched with a rod, and he would be declared free.
A slave might be freed by his master's declaring him so in the presence of friends at home or by his master's simply inviting him to recline at dinner. The word *manumissio* is connected to the words *manus*, meaning *hand*, and *mitto*, *I send*, so it means, literally, *a sending out from the hand*.
[Teachers may use their judgment as to what details to accept for this answer, as others besides those mentioned above are possible, depending on the students' recollection of textbook material and exposure to materials outside the textbook.]   (2 points)

6a A *libertus* was a freedman (freed slave).

6b i He could not stand as a candidate in public elections.
ii He could not become a high-ranking officer in the army.   (2 points)

7a The Romans believed that the spirits of the dead wished to be close to the living, and that they liked to observe the comings and goings of passersby.

7b Wine was a substitute for blood, believed to be the favorite drink of the dead.

7c Epicurus believed that when a person died, the breath that had given that person life dissolved into the air to be lost for ever—hence, that there was no life after death.

8a A *hypocaust* would be used in the baths.

8b Any two details: The hypocaust was a furnace placed below floor level. The floor above a hypocaust system was supported on small brick piles, so that the warm air could circulate freely in the space thus provided, warming the floor above. Later versions of the hypocaust made use of flues in the walls, by means of which warm air could be drawn up into the walls. Charcoal was the fuel usually burned in the furnace of a hypocaust.   (2 points)

9 An *apodyterium* was the changing-room at the baths. / The Romans would remove their clothes here, and leave them with an attendant, before going to bathe.

10a The Nucerians and the Pompeians were the two groups involved in the Great Riot of A.D. 59.

10b The Pompeians were forbidden to hold gladiatorial shows in their amphitheater for ten years following this riot.

11 i net   ii trident   (2 points)

12 Any one detail: A *grammaticus* was the teacher who ran the Roman secondary school / and who introduced the students to famous works of Greek and Roman literature (Homer's epics, Greek tragedies, Vergil's poetry, etc.) along with some history and geography.

13 A *stilus* [i.e. a thin stick of metal, bone, or ivory] was used for writing on *tabulae*.

14 A reed or a goose quill [sharpened at one end and split like a modern pen nib] was used for writing on *papyrus* [with ink made from soot and resin or other substances].

35 points for Part B
Total: 70 points

PART A Understanding the story

Read the following story, and then answer the questions based on it.
Answer all questions on the Answer Sheets provided.

duo frātrēs

in urbe Pompeiīs habitābant duo gladiātōrēs, Pugnāx et Murrānus.
frātrēs erant, et iuvenēs callidissimī et fortissimī. multōs virōs et bēstiās
in pugnā superābant et saepe victōrēs erant. Pugnāx Murrānō frātrī
saepe dīcēbat,
   "ego et tū semper pugnābimus ūsque ad mortem nostram." 5
   ōlim senātor Livinēius Rēgulus spectāculum splendidum ēdēbat.
Pompeiānī et Nūcerīnī quoque ad amphitheātrum Pompeiānum
vēnērunt. itaque magister gladiātōrum, Sulla nōmine, Murrānō et
Pugnācī inquit,
   "hodiē vōs duo contrā murmillōnēs et rētiāriōs et leōnem ingentem 10
pugnātis."
   postquam Murrānus et Pugnāx leōnem et gladiātōrēs facile et
celeriter necāvērunt, magister inquit,
   "nunc inter vōs pugnāte! placetne vōbīs?"
   sed Pugnāx "mihi nōn placet," inquit. 15
   tum magister rīdēbat et rogāvit,
   "num timēs, ō Pugnāx?"
   "nōn timeō sed frātrem meum necāre nōn cupiō."
   "vōs estis servī. cupitisne lībertātem? servus quī superat lībertus est."
   Pugnāx nihil respondit; frātrem spectābat. 20
   iterum magister "timētisne?" inquit.
   nunc Pugnāx et Murrānus trīstēs rem intellēxērunt. quod Murrānus
et Pugnāx magistrum nōn dēlectābant, ūnus eōrum moritūrus erat.
   "ego numquam istī magistrō crēdidī!" susurrāvit Murrānus.
   et nunc turba aliam pugnam quaerēbat. subitō tuba sonuit. Pugnāx 25
et Murrānus in arēnam ambulāvērunt; fortiter Rēgulum salūtāvērunt.
gladiātōrēs gladiōs suōs dēstrīnxērunt; sed multus sanguis nōn fluēbat.
   turba īrāta clāmābat, "cūr nōn pugnātis? cupimus sanguinem!"
   nunc frātrēs dēspērābant. quid manēbat?
   tum Pugnāx frātrī gladium trādidit. 30
   "mē necā, ō frāter! cupiō mortem manibus tuīs."
   itaque Murrānus frātrem interfēcit et clāmōrem horribilem ēmīsit.
tum in eōdem gladiō cecidit mortuus.

dīcēbat	*used to say*
pugnābimus	*we shall fight*
ūsque ad	*up until*
mors: mortem	*death*
nostram	*our*
ēdit	*presents*
itaque	*therefore*
magister gladiātōrum	*trainer (of gladiators)*
nōmine	*by name, named*
contrā	*against*
inter vōs	*between yourselves, with each other*
necāre	*to kill*
lībertas: lībertātem	*freedom*
quī	*who*
trīstis	*sad*
dēlectat	*pleases*
eōrum	*of them*
moritūrus	*going to die*
numquam	*never*
istī	*that*
susurrat	*whispers*
alius	*another*
dēstrīnxit	*unsheathed, drew*
fluit	*flows*
manibus tuīs	*at your hands*
eōdem	*the same*
cecidit	*fell*

PART A Understanding the story

Answer all questions on the Answer Sheets provided.
Answer in complete English sentences (unless otherwise instructed).

1   In the first sentence, find **two** Latin adjectives that describe the brothers. Write down the two Latin words and translate each of them into English.

2   Give proof that the brothers were very good at their craft by translating *multōs virōs et bēstiās in pugnā superābant.* (lines 2–3)

3   What did Pugnax often tell his brother?

4   What did Regulus do once?

5   Who came to watch?

6   Who was Sulla?

7   Who were to be the two gladiators' opponents today?

8   Translate the two adverbs in lines 12 and 13 that describe how Murranus and Pugnax defeated their opponents.

9   What did Sulla tell the brothers after their fights?

10   What was Pugnax' reaction?

11   What reason did the trainer suggest for Pugnax' reaction?

12   What did Pugnax not want to do?

13   Why did the brothers have no choice?

14   Translate: *"servus quī superat lībertus est."* (line 19)

15a   Translate: *"timētisne?"* (line 21)

15b   How do we know that Sulla was talking to both brothers when he said *"timētisne?"*?

16   What conclusion did Pugnax and Murranus come to in line 23 about why Sulla was treating them this way?

17   What did Murranus say about Sulla in line 24?

18   Why was the crowd annoyed?

19   What did Pugnax ask his brother to do?

20   How did Murranus die?

21   Select from the story one example of each of the following:
     i   a verb in the perfect tense
     ii   a noun in the dative singular
     iii   a noun in the accusative plural

22a A *placebo* is an inactive "medicine" given to a patient to fool him or her into thinking it has a beneficial effect. What Latin word in the story is the root for this word?

22b *Sanguine* is an adjective meaning "hopeful" or "confident". What word in the story is its Latin root?

22c *Risible* is an adjective describing things which cause people to laugh. What word in the story is its Latin root?

35 points for Part A

PART B Understanding the background

Answer all questions on the Answer Sheets provided.
Answer in complete English sentences (unless otherwise instructed).

1 What was the name of the type of building where gladiatorial contests were held?

2 How were spectators protected from the sun?

3 How would you have recognized a *murmillō*?

4 What was a *bēstiārius*?

5 How much did a gladiatorial show cost for the spectators?

6 What **two** types of people were usually recruited as gladiators?

7 Study the picture:

7a Why does the kneeling gladiator hold his arm up in this fashion?

7b What did it probably mean if the spectators raised their thumbs toward their chests?

8 What is happening in this picture based on a wall-painting found in Pompeii?

9 What were the items pictured below used for?

10 Study the following pictures. On your Answer Sheet, label the people using the letter beside each of the professions named below.

A *pictor*   B *vēnālīcius*   C *tōnsor*   D *coquus*
E *argentārius*   F *poēta*

i   ii   iii

iv   v   vi

11   Look at the picture:

11a   Where are these scenes taking place?

11b   What is happening in the scene on the left?

11c   What is happening in the scene on the right?

12   Look at the following picture. What are the people doing?

13 Give **two** ways one could become a slave in the ancient world.

14 What was one way of performing the ceremony of manumission?

15 Why did the Romans bury their dead along busy roads?

16 Why was wine often poured into the tombs of the dead?

17 This is the diagram of part of the bathhouse at Pompeii. What was this special heating system called?

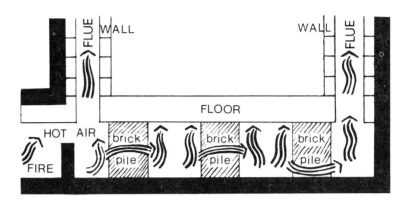

18 What was the most common fuel used to supply the heat?

19 On your Answer Sheet, match the following:

paedagōgus	A	secondary school teacher
ludī magister	B	student escort
grammaticus	C	primary school teacher
rhētor	D	teacher of science and math
	E	teacher after secondary school

20a What name was given to the two senior officials elected yearly to run the lawcourts in Pompeii?

20b What was the name given to the other two officials who ran the public services?

20c What was one of those public services?

35 points for Part B
Total: 70 points

NOMEN ....

PART A Understanding the story

Answer all questions on these sheets.
Answer in complete English sentences (unless otherwise instructed).

1 Latin adjective: _____
   Meaning: _____
   Latin adjective: _____
   Meaning: _____ ☐ 2

2 _____
   _____ ☐ 3

3 _____
   _____ ☐ 1

4 _____ ☐ 1

5 _____
   _____ ☐ 2

6 _____ ☐ 1

7 _____
   _____ ☐ 3

8 i _____
   ii _____ ☐ 2

9 _____ ☐ 1

10 _____ ☐ 1

11 _____ ☐ 1

12 _____ ☐ 1

13 _____ ☐ 1

North American Cambridge Latin Examination: Unit 1 (Form G)

© SCAA Enterprises Limited 1995

NOMEN ....

14 _____

_____ ☐2

15a _____ ☐1

15b _____ ☐1

16 _____ ☐1

17 _____ ☐1

18 _____ ☐1

19 _____ ☐1

20 _____ ☐1

21 i perfect tense verb: _____

  ii dative singular noun: _____

  iii accusative plural noun: _____ ☐3

22a Latin root for *placebo*: _____ ☐1

22b Latin root for *sanguine*: _____ ☐1

22c Latin root for *risible*: _____ ☐1

/35 **points for Part A**

North American Cambridge Latin Examination: Unit 1 (Form G)

© SCAA Enterprises Limited 1995

NOMEN ....

PART B **Understanding the background**

Answer all questions on these sheets.
Answer in complete English sentences (unless otherwise instructed).

1 _____ ☐1

2 _____ ☐1

3 _____ ☐1

4 _____ ☐1

5 _____ ☐1

6 _____
  _____ ☐2

7a _____ ☐1

7b _____ ☐1

8 _____ ☐1

9 _____
  _____ ☐1

10   i   ii   iii   iv   v   vi   ☐6

11a _____ ☐1

11b _____ ☐1

11c _____ ☐1

12 _____ ☐1

13 _____
   _____ ☐2

14 _____
   _____ ☐1

North American Cambridge Latin Examination: Unit 1 (Form G)

© SCAA Enterprises Limited 1995

NOMEN ....

15 _____
_____ ☐1

16 _____
_____ ☐1

17 _____ ☐1

18 _____ ☐1

19 *paedagogus* _____
ludi magister _____
grammaticus _____
rhetor _____ ☐4

20a _____ ☐1

20b _____ ☐1

20c _____ ☐1

/35 **points for Part B**

/35 + /35 = /70 **points total**

North American Cambridge Latin Examination: Unit 1 (Form G)

© SCAA Enterprises Limited 1995

Answer Key

Each question is worth 1 point unless otherwise indicated.

PART A Understanding the story

1. *callidissimi*—very clever; *fortissimi*—very brave (2 points: one point for each word—both the Latin and the English must be correct for the point)
2. They overpowered (would overpower / used to overpower) (1) many men (1) and (wild) animals (1). (3 points total)
3. "You and I shall fight until our death." (can be done as indirect discourse also)
4. He gave/presented a (splendid) show.
5. The Pompeians and the Nucerians came to watch. (2 points: 1 point for each group)
6. He was the (gladiators') trainer.
7. They were to fight against murmillones and retiarii and a huge lion. (3 points: 1 point for each opponent)
8. "easily"; "quickly" (2 points)
9. He told them they were now to fight each other.
10. He didn't like it.
11. He thought Pugnax was afraid.
12. He did not want to kill his brother.
13. They were slaves.
14. The slave who wins/conquers/overpowers (1) is a freedman / is free(d) (1). (2 points total)
15a. "Are you afraid?"
15b. *timetis* is 2nd person **plural** / the *-tis* ending is "you" plural, etc.
16. The trainer did not like them.
17. He said that he had never trusted him.
18. There was no blood.
19. He asked him to kill him.
20. He fell on his own sword.
21.
    i *venerunt* (line 8); *necaverunt* (line 13); *rogavit* (line 16); *respondit* (line 20); *intellexerunt* (line 22); *credidi* (line 24); *susurravit* (line 24); *sonuit* (line 25); *ambulaverunt* (line 26); *salutaverunt* (line 26); *destrinxerunt* (line 27); *tradidit* (line 30); *interfecit* (line 32); *emisit* (line 32); *cecidit* (line 33)
    ii *Murrano* (lines 3 & 8); *fratri* (lines 3 & 30); *Pugnaci* (line 9); *magistro* (line 24) (Also allow *gladio* (line 33) if someone gives it, since they have not officially met the ablative yet.)
    iii *viros* (line 2); *bestias* (line 2); *murmillones* (line 10); *retiarios* (line 10); *gladiatores* (line 12); *gladios* (line 27)   (3 points)
22a. *placet* (lines 14 & 15)
22b. *sanguis* (line 27); *sanguinem* (line 28)
22c. *ridebat* (line 16)

35 points for Part A

PART B Understanding the background

1. It was called an amphitheater (or *amphitheatrum*).
2. Awnings were erected.
3. He wore a crest shaped like a fish on his helmet / he had a fish design on his armor.
4. He was a beast-fighter (a gladiator that fought animals).
5. It was free.
6. Slaves or condemned criminals were recruited as gladiators. (2 points)
7a. He is asking for mercy.
7b. They wanted the death of the gladiator.
8. A riot is taking place (students may mention the Nucerians, but do not need to).
9. They are admission tickets to the theater (students may also mention that they indicated the proper entrance or seating area).
10. i D; ii F; iii C; iv B; v E; vi A (6 points)
11a. These scenes are taking place in the forum.
11b. A man is selling articles of metal ware.
11c. A man is selling shoes.
12. They are reading notice boards (in the forum).
13. Any two of: You might be born into slavery / captured in war / captured by pirates. (2 points)
14. Any one of: You could take your slave to a judge and say you didn't really own the slave / declare him free in the presence of friends / invite him to recline on the couch at dinner.
15. They wished to give them companionship. / The dead liked to be near what was going on. / etc.
16. It was a convenient substitute for blood (the favorite drink of the dead).
17. It was called a hypocaust.
18. The most common fuel was charcoal.
19.
    paedagogus   B
    ludi magister C
    grammaticus   A
    rhetor   E
20a. They were called *duoviri* (duovirs).
20b. They were called *aediles*.
20c. Any one of: public markets, police force, baths, places of public entertainment, water supply, sewers.

35 points for Part B
Total: 70 points